The MILLIONAIRE BLUEPRINT

How To Turn $100 Into $1,000,000 Within One Year

Christopher & Stacy Mitchell

The Millionaire Blueprint
How To Turn $100 Into $1,000,000 Within One Year

Copyright © 2021 Lavish Life Inc.

ISBN: 9798728094951

Imprint: Independently published

Printed in the United States of America

This Year

Belongs

To

_____

The Difference A Year Can Make!

*"Dishonest money dwindles away,
but he who gathers money little
by little makes it grow."*
Proverbs 13:11

Welcome

TO THE FAMILY

Hello Friend. We want to welcome you into the *Change Your Life* Family and we're excited to present to you the 3% Guaranteed Millionaire Blueprint. This blueprint will teach you how to turn just $100 into $1,000,000 within one year. We created this blueprint to encourage you and guide you on your journey to a life that will be forever changed.

It's a proven fact that the way to create lasting change is to do it one step at a time. That is why the entire focus of this blueprint is to simply take one step forward, reaching one small goal everyday.

This journey does not require anything superhuman. It simply requires a commitment to consistently take one step at a time, achieving a small 3% profit goal every single day.

The main goal is not reaching the $1,000,000 but that will be a nice bonus! The main goal is to teach you a process that will help you achieve any goal by using a different approach. That approach is breaking down a large goal into small, attainable daily goals. Success is achieved one small step at a time.

We believe the next 365 days will *Change Your Life*. So, Dream Big, Stay Committed and Focus on Winning each day!

Love,
Christopher & Stacy Mitchell

Dream Big

Live Life By Design, Not Default, CREATE IT

You are the artist of your life. You were designed to Dream Big and achieve great things. Every great achievement began in the mind of one person. Take some time and allow yourself to ask, "What if?"

What dreams have you let go of or buried under the chaos of life? It is time to re-ignite those dreams and fan the flames. Life is too short to let them go!

Take this time to write down your dreams, big and small using the Vision Board on the next page.

Every dream must take the form of a plan. Your dreams will not just happen. The old saying "You get what you plan for" is so true!

We have created this blueprint as your step by step plan to achieving your goals!

Vision Board

"Where there is no vision, the people perish."
Proverbs 29:18

List your Dreams Big and Small Below

3% Strategy

The most important thing you need to achieving any goal is a *Plan.* The plan of this blueprint is based upon the strategy of COMPOUND INVESTING. Here is the breakdown of how The Millionaire Blueprint works.

We are going to share with you how you can *Change Your Life* financially with small daily 3% increments. We are starting with $100. Each day you will grow your total daily balance by only 3%. Each day your balance will grow little by little. Leave ALL of the money in what we call your Piggy Bank Account. Don't touch it and watch what happens! On day 365 you will have acquired well over 1 Million Dollars. It's important to develop a disciplined approach and follow the process day by day. Not only are you growing your Piggy Bank Account each day but you are also Retraining Your Brain to be mentally prepared for what is to come. The daily goal amount starts out small, but as the months progress it also increases. If you follow the process day by day, your money will grow but so will your mindset. Mastering your mindset is the key to having success in life.

How you achieve your daily 3% goal will be up to you. If you currently only have one stream of income and need help creating more, we can help! Contact us and we can show you how.

Accountability

You alone are responsible for the success or failure of reaching your goals. A crucial component to having success in reaching your goals is *Accountability*.

One way to help achieve this is to establish *Accountability Buddies.* Making a commitment to someone else creates accountability, pushing you to show up every day and take action even if you don't feel like it. Find a buddy or buddies to walk this journey with you.

If you want a community to walk this journey with, contact us about joining our Inner Circle. It is filled with people from all over the world who want to *Change Their Life* just like you. It is a community filled with mentorship, weekly live coaching, strategies to implement new income streams, accountability and new friendships. Contact us to learn more.

Accountability Buddies

1.

2.

3.

Commitment Pledge

If you want the remaining years of your life to look different than your life looks today, you need to make different decisions. Make a pledge to yourself to fully commit to reaching your daily goals for the next 365 days and see the difference a year can make in your life.

Life happens! The routine demands of life will carry on and unexpected circumstances may show up out of nowhere and try to derail you off course. When these things occur, we all face the urge to give up. Don't do it! Quitting is a habit and it's time to break that habit!

Commitment Pledge:

"This is my time, my life, my moment of truth. I am committing to the next 365 days to taking my daily step and reaching my daily goal to create a new result in my life. I refuse to allow any fear, limiting beliefs, circumstances, or anything else in my life stop me from making this happen. I will remain focused on my goal and take full responsibility for my results."

Signature:

Today's Date:

Change Your Life

How To Use The Blueprint

- This blueprint is designed to be your daily step by step guide on your journey from $100 to $1,000,000.

- Each day you will have your 3% Daily Financial Goal Amount listed. If you achieve the daily goal amount, check the box marked Achieved. ☑

- On each day you will also see a Piggy Bank Balance which includes the initial investment of $100 plus all of the accumulated earnings to date.

- Every 30 Days there will be a 30 Day check in. This is your time to do some self evaluation on how your journey is going, make any adjustments that need to be made and celebrate your achievements!

- This blueprint is a guide to help you start reaching your goals by achieving small daily wins. If you don't hit the goal each day or it takes you longer than 365 days, that is ok! This blueprint is not all about making money, it's about teaching you a winning approach that you can implement to achieve any goal. It helps you stay committed and be consistent with a plan. Consistency is what will *Change Your Life*.

LET'S DO THIS!

Month One

Investment $100

DAY 1	Daily 3% Goal $3.00	Piggy Bank Balance $103.00
Date:	Achieved ☐	
DAY 2	Daily 3% Goal $3.09	Piggy Bank Balance $106.09
Date:	Achieved ☐	
DAY 3	Daily 3% Goal $3.18	Piggy Bank Balance $109.27
Date:	Achieved ☐	

Month One

DAY 4	Daily 3% Goal	
	$3.28	Piggy Bank Balance
Date:	Achieved ☐	**$112.55**

DAY 5	Daily 3% Goal	
	$3.38	Piggy Bank Balance
Date:	Achieved ☐	**$115.93**

DAY 6	Daily 3% Goal	
	$3.48	Piggy Bank Balance
Date:	Achieved ☐	**$119.41**

Month One

DAY 7	Daily 3% Goal	
	$3.58	Piggy Bank Balance
Date:	Achieved ☐	$122.99

DAY 8	Daily 3% Goal	
	$3.69	Piggy Bank Balance
Date:	Achieved ☐	$126.68

DAY 9	Daily 3% Goal	
	$3.80	Piggy Bank Balance
Date:	Achieved ☐	$130.48

Month One

DAY 10	Daily 3% Goal $3.91 Achieved ☐ Date:	Piggy Bank Balance $134.39
DAY 11	Daily 3% Goal $4.03 Achieved ☐ Date:	Piggy Bank Balance $138.42
DAY 12	Daily 3% Goal $4.15 Achieved ☐ Date:	Piggy Bank Balance $142.58

Month One

DAY 13

Daily 3% Goal

$4.28

Achieved ☐

Date:

Piggy Bank Balance

$146.85

DAY 14

Daily 3% Goal

$4.41

Achieved ☐

Date:

Piggy Bank Balance

$151.26

DAY 15

Daily 3% Goal

$4.54

Achieved ☐

Date:

Piggy Bank Balance

$155.80

Month One

DAY 16	Daily 3% Goal $4.67 Achieved ☐	 Piggy Bank Balance $160.47
Date:		
DAY 17	Daily 3% Goal $4.81 Achieved ☐	 Piggy Bank Balance $165.28
Date:		
DAY 18	Daily 3% Goal $4.96 Achieved ☐	 Piggy Bank Balance $170.24
Date:		

Month One

DAY 19	Daily 3% Goal	
	$5.11	
	Achieved ☐	Piggy Bank Balance
Date:		$175.35

DAY 20	Daily 3% Goal	
	$5.26	
	Achieved ☐	Piggy Bank Balance
Date:		$180.61

DAY 21	Daily 3% Goal	
	$5.42	
	Achieved ☐	Piggy Bank Balance
Date:		$186.03

Month One

DAY 22	Daily 3% Goal $5.58	Piggy Bank Balance
Date:	Achieved ☐	$191.61

DAY 23	Daily 3% Goal $5.75	Piggy Bank Balance
Date:	Achieved ☐	$197.36

DAY 24	Daily 3% Goal $5.92	Piggy Bank Balance
Date:	Achieved ☐	$203.28

Month One

DAY 25	Daily 3% Goal $6.10	Piggy Bank Balance
Date:	Achieved ☐	$209.38

DAY 26	Daily 3% Goal $6.28	Piggy Bank Balance
Date:	Achieved ☐	$215.66

DAY 27	Daily 3% Goal $6.47	Piggy Bank Balance
Date:	Achieved ☐	$222.13

Month One

DAY 28	Daily 3% Goal	
	$6.66	
Date:	Achieved ☐	Piggy Bank Balance **$228.79**

DAY 29	Daily 3% Goal	
	$6.86	
Date:	Achieved ☐	Piggy Bank Balance **$235.66**

DAY 30	Daily 3% Goal	
	$7.07	
Date:	Achieved ☐	Piggy Bank Balance **$242.73**

Notes

"Inch by inch anything's a cinch. Yard by yard it will be too hard"

30 Day
REVIEW

How many days did you reach you Daily Goal?
If you did not reach your goal each day, identify the obstacles you faced.

1.
2.
3.

What action steps need to be taken to overcome the obstacles and get you back on track?

1.
2.
3.

Celebrate Your Victories!
List 1 or 2 things you will do this week to reward yourself for a job well done!

1.
2.

Month Two

DAY 31	Daily 3% Goal $7.28	
Date:	Achieved ☐	Piggy Bank Balance $250.01

DAY 32	Daily 3% Goal $7.50	
Date:	Achieved ☐	Piggy Bank Balance $257.51

DAY 33	Daily 3% Goal $7.73	
Date:	Achieved ☐	Piggy Bank Balance $265.23

Month Two

DAY 34	Daily 3% Goal $7.96 Achieved ☐	Piggy Bank Balance $273.19
Date:		
DAY 35	Daily 3% Goal $8.20 Achieved ☐	Piggy Bank Balance $281.39
Date:		
DAY 36	Daily 3% Goal $8.44 Achieved ☐	Piggy Bank Balance $289.83
Date:		

Month Two

DAY 37	Daily 3% Goal $8.69	
Date:	Achieved ☐	Piggy Bank Balance $298.52
DAY 38	Daily 3% Goal $8.96	
Date:	Achieved ☐	Piggy Bank Balance $307.48
DAY 39	Daily 3% Goal $9.22	
Date:	Achieved ☐	Piggy Bank Balance $316.70

Month Two

DAY 40	Daily 3% Goal **$9.50** Achieved ☐	 Piggy Bank Balance **$326.20**
Date:		
DAY 41	Daily 3% Goal **$9.79** Achieved ☐	 Piggy Bank Balance **$335.99**
Date:		
DAY 42	Daily 3% Goal **$10.08** Achieved ☐	 Piggy Bank Balance **$346.07**
Date:		

Month Two

DAY 43	Daily 3% Goal	
	$10.38	
	Achieved ☐	Piggy Bank Balance
Date:		**$356.45**

DAY 44	Daily 3% Goal	
	$10.69	
	Achieved ☐	Piggy Bank Balance
Date:		**$367.15**

DAY 45	Daily 3% Goal	
	$11.01	
	Achieved ☐	Piggy Bank Balance
Date:		**$378.16**

Month Two

DAY 46	Daily 3% Goal $11.34 Achieved ☐	 Piggy Bank Balance **$389.50**
Date:		
DAY 47	Daily 3% Goal $11.69 Achieved ☐	 Piggy Bank Balance **$401.19**
Date:		
DAY 48	Daily 3% Goal $12.04 Achieved ☐	 Piggy Bank Balance **$413.23**
Date:		

Month Two

DAY 49	Daily 3% Goal $12.40 Achieved ☐	Piggy Bank Balance **$425.62**
Date:		
DAY 50	Daily 3% Goal $12.77 Achieved ☐	Piggy Bank Balance **$438.39**
Date:		
DAY 51	Daily 3% Goal $13.15 Achieved ☐	Piggy Bank Balance **$451.54**
Date:		

Month Two

DAY 52	Daily 3% Goal $13.55	
	Achieved ☐	Piggy Bank Balance **$465.09**
Date:		

DAY 53	Daily 3% Goal $13.95	
	Achieved ☐	Piggy Bank Balance **$479.04**
Date:		

DAY 54	Daily 3% Goal $14.37	
	Achieved ☐	Piggy Bank Balance **$493.41**
Date:		

Month Two

DAY 55	Daily 3% Goal	
	$14.80	
Date:	Achieved ☐	Piggy Bank Balance **$508.21**

DAY 56	Daily 3% Goal	
	$15.25	
Date:	Achieved ☐	Piggy Bank Balance **$523.46**

DAY 57	Daily 3% Goal	
	$15.70	
Date:	Achieved ☐	Piggy Bank Balance **$539.17**

Month Two

DAY 58	Daily 3% Goal	
	$16.17	**Piggy Bank Balance**
Date:	Achieved ☐	**$555.34**

DAY 59	Daily 3% Goal	
	$16.66	**Piggy Bank Balance**
Date:	Achieved ☐	**$572.00**

DAY 60	Daily 3% Goal	
	$17.16	**Piggy Bank Balance**
Date:	Achieved ☐	**$589.16**

Notes

"Change the way you look at things, and the things you look at change." -Wayne Dyer

60 Day
REVIEW

How many days did you reach you Daily Goal?
If you did not reach your goal each day, identify the obstacles you faced.

1.
2.
3.

What action steps need to be taken to overcome the obstacles and get you back on track?

1.
2.
3.

Celebrate Your Victories!
List 1 or 2 things you will do this week to reward yourself for a job well done!

1.
2.

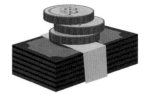

Month Three

DAY 61	Daily 3% Goal $17.67 Achieved ☐	Piggy Bank Balance $606.84
Date:		
DAY 62	Daily 3% Goal $18.21 Achieved ☐	Piggy Bank Balance $625.04
Date:		
DAY 63	Daily 3% Goal $18.75 Achieved ☐	Piggy Bank Balance $643.79
Date:		

Month Three

DAY 64 Date:	Daily 3% Goal **$19.31** Achieved ☐	 Piggy Bank Balance **$663.11**
DAY 65 Date:	Daily 3% Goal **$19.89** Achieved ☐	 Piggy Bank Balance **$683.00**
DAY 66 Date:	Daily 3% Goal **$20.49** Achieved ☐	 Piggy Bank Balance **$703.49**

Month Three

DAY 67	Daily 3% Goal $21.10	Piggy Bank Balance $724.59
Date:	Achieved ☐	
DAY 68	Daily 3% Goal $21.74	Piggy Bank Balance $746.33
Date:	Achieved ☐	
DAY 69	Daily 3% Goal $22.39	Piggy Bank Balance $768.72
Date:	Achieved ☐	

Month Three

DAY 70 Date:	Daily 3% Goal **$23.06** Achieved ☐	 Piggy Bank Balance **$791.78**
DAY 71 Date:	Daily 3% Goal **$23.75** Achieved ☐	 Piggy Bank Balance **$815.54**
DAY 72 Date:	Daily 3% Goal **$24.47** Achieved ☐	 Piggy Bank Balance **$840.00**

Month Three

DAY 73 | Daily 3% Goal |
$25.20
Achieved ☐ | Piggy Bank Balance
Date: | | $865.20

DAY 74 | Daily 3% Goal |
$25.96
Achieved ☐ | Piggy Bank Balance
Date: | | $891.16

DAY 75 | Daily 3% Goal |
$26.73
Achieved ☐ | Piggy Bank Balance
Date: | | $917.89

Month Three

DAY 76 Date:	Daily 3% Goal $27.54 Achieved ☐	Piggy Bank Balance $945.43
DAY 77 Date:	Daily 3% Goal $28.36 Achieved ☐	Piggy Bank Balance $973.79
DAY 78 Date:	Daily 3% Goal $29.21 Achieved ☐	Piggy Bank Balance $1,003.01

Month Three

DAY 79 | Daily 3% Goal |

$30.09

Achieved ☐

Date:

Piggy Bank Balance

$1,033.10

DAY 80 | Daily 3% Goal |

$30.99

Achieved ☐

Date:

Piggy Bank Balance

$1,064.09

DAY 81 | Daily 3% Goal |

$31.92

Achieved ☐

Date:

Piggy Bank Balance

$1,096.01

Month Three

DAY 82	Daily 3% Goal	
	$32.88	Piggy Bank Balance
Date:	Achieved ☐	**$1,128.89**

DAY 83	Daily 3% Goal	
	$33.87	Piggy Bank Balance
Date:	Achieved ☐	**$1,162.76**

DAY 84	Daily 3% Goal	
	$34.88	Piggy Bank Balance
Date:	Achieved ☐	**$1,197.64**

Month Three

DAY 85	Daily 3% Goal **$35.93** Achieved ☐	Piggy Bank Balance **$1,233.57**
Date:		
DAY 86	Daily 3% Goal **$37.01** Achieved ☐	Piggy Bank Balance **$1,270.58**
Date:		
DAY 87	Daily 3% Goal **$38.12** Achieved ☐	Piggy Bank Balance **$1,308.70**
Date:		

Month Three

DAY 88	Daily 3% Goal	
	$39.26	
Date:	Achieved ☐	Piggy Bank Balance $1,347.96

DAY 89	Daily 3% Goal	
	$40.44	
Date:	Achieved ☐	Piggy Bank Balance $1,388.39

DAY 90	Daily 3% Goal	
	$41.65	
Date:	Achieved ☐	Piggy Bank Balance $1,430.05

Notes

"Look at what everyone else in the world is doing, and do the exact opposite."

90 Day
REVIEW

How many days did you reach you Daily Goal?
If you did not reach your goal each day, identify the
obstacles you faced.

1.

2.

3.

What action steps need to be taken to overcome the
obstacles and get you back on track?

1.

2.

3.

Celebrate Your Victories!
List 1 or 2 things you will do this week to reward
yourself for a job well done!

1.

2.

Month Four

DAY 91	Daily 3% Goal $42.90 Achieved ☐	Piggy Bank Balance $1,472.95
Date:		
DAY 92	Daily 3% Goal $44.19 Achieved ☐	Piggy Bank Balance $1,517.14
Date:		
DAY 93	Daily 3% Goal $45.51 Achieved ☐	Piggy Bank Balance $1,562.65
Date:		

Month Four

DAY 94	Daily 3% Goal	
	$46.88	
Date:	Achieved ☐	Piggy Bank Balance $1,609.53
DAY 95	Daily 3% Goal	
	$48.29	
Date:	Achieved ☐	Piggy Bank Balance $1,657.82
DAY 96	Daily 3% Goal	
	$49.73	
Date:	Achieved ☐	Piggy Bank Balance $1,707.55

Month Four

DAY 97	Daily 3% Goal $51.23 Achieved ☐	Piggy Bank Balance **$1,758.78**
Date:		
DAY 98	Daily 3% Goal $52.76 Achieved ☐	Piggy Bank Balance **$1,811.54**
Date:		
DAY 99	Daily 3% Goal $54.35 Achieved ☐	Piggy Bank Balance **$1,865.89**
Date:		

Month Four

DAY 100	Daily 3% Goal	
	$55.98	
	Achieved ☐	Piggy Bank Balance
Date:		$1,921.86
DAY 101	Daily 3% Goal	
	$57.66	
	Achieved ☐	Piggy Bank Balance
Date:		$1,979.52
DAY 102	Daily 3% Goal	
	$59.39	
	Achieved ☐	Piggy Bank Balance
Date:		$2,038.90

Month Four

DAY 103	Daily 3% Goal $61.17 Achieved ☐	Piggy Bank Balance $2,100.07
Date:		
DAY 104	Daily 3% Goal $63.00 Achieved ☐	Piggy Bank Balance $2,163.07
Date:		
DAY 105	Daily 3% Goal $64.89 Achieved ☐	Piggy Bank Balance $2,227.97
Date:		

Month Four

DAY 106	Daily 3% Goal	
	$66.84	Piggy Bank Balance
Date:	Achieved ☐	**$2,294.81**

DAY 107	Daily 3% Goal	
	$68.84	Piggy Bank Balance
Date:	Achieved ☐	**$2,363.65**

DAY 108	Daily 3% Goal	
	$70.91	Piggy Bank Balance
Date:	Achieved ☐	**$2,434.56**

Month Four

DAY 109	Daily 3% Goal $73.04	
Date:	Achieved ☐	Piggy Bank Balance $2,507.60

DAY 110	Daily 3% Goal $75.23	
Date:	Achieved ☐	Piggy Bank Balance $2,582.82

DAY 111	Daily 3% Goal $77.48	
Date:	Achieved ☐	Piggy Bank Balance $2,660.31

Month Four

DAY 112	Daily 3% Goal $79.81 Achieved ☐ Date:	Piggy Bank Balance $2,740.12
DAY 113	Daily 3% Goal $82.20 Achieved ☐ Date:	Piggy Bank Balance $2,822.32
DAY 114	Daily 3% Goal $84.67 Achieved ☐ Date:	Piggy Bank Balance $2,906.99

Month Four

DAY 115	Daily 3% Goal	
	$87.21	
	Achieved ☐	Piggy Bank Balance
Date:		$2,994.20

DAY 116	Daily 3% Goal	
	$89.83	
	Achieved ☐	Piggy Bank Balance
Date:		$3,084.03

DAY 117	Daily 3% Goal	
	$92.52	
	Achieved ☐	Piggy Bank Balance
Date:		$3,176.55

Month Four

DAY 118 Date:	Daily 3% Goal **$95.30** Achieved ☐	Piggy Bank Balance **$3,271.84**
DAY 119 Date:	Daily 3% Goal **$98.16** Achieved ☐	Piggy Bank Balance **$3,370.00**
DAY 120 Date:	Daily 3% Goal **$101.10** Achieved ☐	Piggy Bank Balance **$3,471.10**

Notes

Watch Your Words!
"Your words are seeds and will manifest in your life."

120 Day
REVIEW

How many days did you reach you Daily Goal?
If you did not reach your goal each day, identify the
obstacles you faced.

1.
2.
3.

What action steps need to be taken to overcome the
obstacles and get you back on track?

1.
2.
3.

Celebrate Your Victories!
List 1 or 2 things you will do this week to reward
yourself for a job well done!

1.
2.

Month Five

DAY 121 | Daily 3% Goal

$104.13

Achieved ☐

Piggy Bank Balance

$3,575.23

Date:

DAY 122 | Daily 3% Goal

$107.26

Achieved ☐

Piggy Bank Balance

$3,682.49

Date:

DAY 123 | Daily 3% Goal

$110.47

Achieved ☐

Piggy Bank Balance

$3,792.96

Date:

Month Five

DAY 124	Daily 3% Goal	
	$113.79	
	Achieved ☐	Piggy Bank Balance
Date:		$3,906.75

DAY 125	Daily 3% Goal	
	$117.20	
	Achieved ☐	Piggy Bank Balance
Date:		$4,023.95

DAY 126	Daily 3% Goal	
	$120.72	
	Achieved ☐	Piggy Bank Balance
Date:		$4,144.67

Month Five

DAY 127	Daily 3% Goal $124.34 Achieved ☐	 Piggy Bank Balance **$4,269.01**
Date:		
DAY 128	Daily 3% Goal $128.07 Achieved ☐	 Piggy Bank Balance **$4,39708**
Date:		
DAY 129	Daily 3% Goal $131.91 Achieved ☐	 Piggy Bank Balance **$4,529.00**
Date:		

Month Five

DAY 130 Date:	Daily 3% Goal $135.87 Achieved ☐	 Piggy Bank Balance **$4,664.87**
DAY 131 Date:	Daily 3% Goal $139.95 Achieved ☐	 Piggy Bank Balance **$4,804.81**
DAY 132 Date:	Daily 3% Goal $144.14 Achieved ☐	 Piggy Bank Balance **$4,948.96**

Month Five

DAY 133	Daily 3% Goal	
	$148.47	
		Piggy Bank Balance
	Achieved ☐	$5,097.43
Date:		
DAY 134	Daily 3% Goal	
	$152.92	
		Piggy Bank Balance
	Achieved ☐	$5,250.35
Date:		
DAY 135	Daily 3% Goal	
	$157.51	
		Piggy Bank Balance
	Achieved ☐	$5,407.86
Date:		

Month Five

DAY 136	Daily 3% Goal	
	$162.24	
Date:	Achieved ☐	Piggy Bank Balance $5,570.09

DAY 137	Daily 3% Goal	
	$167.10	
Date:	Achieved ☐	Piggy Bank Balance $5,737.20

DAY 138	Daily 3% Goal	
	$172.12	
Date:	Achieved ☐	Piggy Bank Balance $5,909.31

Month Five

DAY 139	Daily 3% Goal $177.28	
	Achieved ☐	Piggy Bank Balance $6,086.59
Date:		
DAY 140	Daily 3% Goal $182.60	
	Achieved ☐	Piggy Bank Balance $6,269.19
Date:		
DAY 141	Daily 3% Goal $188.08	
	Achieved ☐	Piggy Bank Balance $6,457.27
Date:		

Month Five

DAY 142	Daily 3% Goal	
	$193.72	
Date:	Achieved ☐	**Piggy Bank Balance** $6,650.98
DAY 143	Daily 3% Goal	
	$199.53	
Date:	Achieved ☐	**Piggy Bank Balance** $6,850.51
DAY 144	Daily 3% Goal	
	$205.52	
Date:	Achieved ☐	**Piggy Bank Balance** $7,056.03

Month Five

DAY 145	Daily 3% Goal	
	$211.68	
	Achieved ☐	Piggy Bank Balance
Date:		$7,267.71
DAY 146	Daily 3% Goal	
	$218.03	
	Achieved ☐	Piggy Bank Balance
Date:		$7,485.74
DAY 147	Daily 3% Goal	
	$224.57	
	Achieved ☐	Piggy Bank Balance
Date:		$7,710.31

Month Five

Day 148	Daily 3% Goal $231.31	
	Achieved ☐	Piggy Bank Balance **$7,941.62**
Date:		

Day 149	Daily 3% Goal $238.25	
	Achieved ☐	Piggy Bank Balance **$8,179.87**
Date:		

Day 150	Daily 3% Goal $245.40	
	Achieved ☐	Piggy Bank Balance **$8,425.27**
Date:		

Notes

"All the flowers of tomorrow are in the seeds of today."
- Ancient Proverb

150 Day
REVIEW

How many days did you reach you Daily Goal?
If you did not reach your goal each day, identify the obstacles you faced.

1.
2.
3.

What action steps need to be taken to overcome the obstacles and get you back on track?

1.
2.
3.

Celebrate Your Victories!
List 1 or 2 things you will do this week to reward yourself for a job well done!

1.
2.

Month Six

DAY 151	Daily 3% Goal $252.76 Achieved ☐	Piggy Bank Balance $8,678.03
Date:		
DAY 152	Daily 3% Goal $260.34 Achieved ☐	Piggy Bank Balance $8,938.37
Date:		
DAY 153	Daily 3% Goal $268.15 Achieved ☐	Piggy Bank Balance $9,206.52
Date:		

Month Six

DAY 154	Daily 3% Goal $276.20 Achieved ☐	 Piggy Bank Balance **$9,482.71**
Date:		
DAY 155	Daily 3% Goal $284.48 Achieved ☐	 Piggy Bank Balance **$9,767.19**
Date:		
DAY 156	Daily 3% Goal $293.02 Achieved ☐	 Piggy Bank Balance **$10,060.21**
Date:		

Month Six

DAY 157	Daily 3% Goal $301.81 Achieved ☐	 Piggy Bank Balance $10,362.02
Date:		
DAY 158	Daily 3% Goal $310.86 Achieved ☐	 Piggy Bank Balance $10,672.88
Date:		
DAY 159	Daily 3% Goal $320.19 Achieved ☐	 Piggy Bank Balance $10,993.06
Date:		

Month Six

DAY 160	Daily 3% Goal	
	$329.79	
Date:	Achieved ☐	Piggy Bank Balance $11,322.86

DAY 161	Daily 3% Goal	
	$339.69	
Date:	Achieved ☐	Piggy Bank Balance $11,662.54

DAY 162	Daily 3% Goal	
	$349.88	
Date:	Achieved ☐	Piggy Bank Balance $12,012.42

Month Six

DAY 163	Daily 3% Goal **$360.37** Achieved ☐	 Piggy Bank Balance **$12,372.79**
Date:		
DAY 164	Daily 3% Goal **$371.18** Achieved ☐	 Piggy Bank Balance **$12,743.97**
Date:		
DAY 165	Daily 3% Goal **$382.32** Achieved ☐	 Piggy Bank Balance **$13,126.29**
Date:		

Month Six

DAY 166	Daily 3% Goal	
	$393.79	 **Piggy Bank Balance**
Date:	Achieved ☐	**$13,520.08**

DAY 167	Daily 3% Goal	
	$405.60	 **Piggy Bank Balance**
Date:	Achieved ☐	**$13,925.68**

DAY 168	Daily 3% Goal	
	$417.77	 **Piggy Bank Balance**
Date:	Achieved ☐	**$14,343.45**

Month Six

DAY 169

Daily 3% Goal

$430.30

Achieved ☐

Date:

Piggy Bank Balance

$14,773.76

DAY 170

Daily 3% Goal

$443.21

Achieved ☐

Date:

Piggy Bank Balance

$15,216.97

DAY 171

Daily 3% Goal

$456.51

Achieved ☐

Date:

Piggy Bank Balance

$15,673.48

Month Six

DAY 172	Daily 3% Goal	
	$470.20	
	Achieved ☐	Piggy Bank Balance
Date:		**$16,143.68**

DAY 173	Daily 3% Goal	
	$484.31	
	Achieved ☐	Piggy Bank Balance
Date:		**$16,627.99**

DAY 174	Daily 3% Goal	
	$498.84	
	Achieved ☐	Piggy Bank Balance
Date:		**$17,126.83**

Month Six

DAY 172
Daily 3% Goal

$470.20

Achieved ☐

Piggy Bank Balance

$16,143.68

Date:

DAY 173
Daily 3% Goal

$484.31

Achieved ☐

Piggy Bank Balance

$16,627.99

Date:

DAY 174
Daily 3% Goal

$498.84

Achieved ☐

Piggy Bank Balance

$17,126.83

Date:

Month Six

DAY 175	Daily 3% Goal	
	$513.81	
Date:	Achieved ☐	Piggy Bank Balance $17,640.64

DAY 176	Daily 3% Goal	
	$529.22	
Date:	Achieved ☐	Piggy Bank Balance $18,169.86

DAY 177	Daily 3% Goal	
	$545.10	
Date:	Achieved ☐	Piggy Bank Balance $18,714.95

Month Six

DAY 178	Daily 3% Goal $561.45 Achieved ☐	 Piggy Bank Balance $19,276.40
Date:		
DAY 179	Daily 3% Goal $578.29 Achieved ☐	 Piggy Bank Balance $19,854.70
Date:		
DAY 180	Daily 3% Goal $595.64 Achieved ☐	 Piggy Bank Balance $20,450.34
Date:		

Notes

"You are never too old to set another goal or to dream a NEW DREAM." - C.S Lewis

180 Day
REVIEW

How many days did you reach you Daily Goal?
If you did not reach your goal each day, identify the
obstacles you faced.

1.
2.
3.

What action steps need to be taken to overcome the
obstacles and get you back on track?

1.
2.
3.

Celebrate Your Victories!
List 1 or 2 things you will do this week to reward
yourself for a job well done!

1.
2.

Month Seven

DAY 181	Daily 3% Goal	
	$613.51	
	Achieved ☐	Piggy Bank Balance
Date:		**$21,063.85**

DAY 182	Daily 3% Goal	
	$631.92	
	Achieved ☐	Piggy Bank Balance
Date:		**$21,695.76**

DAY 183	Daily 3% Goal	
	$650.87	
	Achieved ☐	Piggy Bank Balance
Date:		**$22,346.63**

Month Seven

DAY 184

Daily 3% Goal

$670.40

Achieved ☐

Date:

Piggy Bank Balance

$23,017.03

DAY 185

Daily 3% Goal

$690.51

Achieved ☐

Date:

Piggy Bank Balance

$23,707.54

DAY 186

Daily 3% Goal

$711.23

Achieved ☐

Date:

Piggy Bank Balance

$24,418.77

Month Seven

DAY 187	Daily 3% Goal	
	$732.56	Piggy Bank Balance
Date:	Achieved ☐	**$25,151.33**

DAY 188	Daily 3% Goal	
	$754.54	Piggy Bank Balance
Date:	Achieved ☐	**$25,905.87**

DAY 189	Daily 3% Goal	
	$777.18	Piggy Bank Balance
Date:	Achieved ☐	**$26,683.05**

Month Seven

DAY 190   Daily 3% Goal

$800.49

Achieved ☐

Piggy Bank Balance

$27,483.54

Date:

DAY 191   Daily 3% Goal

$824.51

Achieved ☐

Piggy Bank Balance

$28,308.05

Date:

DAY 192   Daily 3% Goal

$849.24

Achieved ☐

Piggy Bank Balance

$29,157.29

Date:

Month Seven

Day 193

Daily 3% Goal

$874.72

Achieved ☐

Piggy Bank Balance

$30,032.01

Date:

Day 194

Daily 3% Goal

$900.96

Achieved ☐

Piggy Bank Balance

$30,932.97

Date:

Day 195

Daily 3% Goal

$927.99

Achieved ☐

Piggy Bank Balance

$31,860.96

Date:

Month Seven

DAY 196	Daily 3% Goal	
	$955.83	Piggy Bank Balance
Date:	Achieved ☐	**$32,816.79**

DAY 197	Daily 3% Goal	
	$984.50	Piggy Bank Balance
Date:	Achieved ☐	**$33,801.29**

DAY 198	Daily 3% Goal	
	$1,014.04	Piggy Bank Balance
Date:	Achieved ☐	**$34,815.33**

Month Seven

DAY 199	Daily 3% Goal **$1,044.46** Achieved ☐	 Piggy Bank Balance **$35,859.79**
Date:		
DAY 200	Daily 3% Goal **$1,075.79** Achieved ☐	 Piggy Bank Balance **$36,935.58**
Date:		
DAY 201	Daily 3% Goal **$1,108.07** Achieved ☐	 Piggy Bank Balance **$38,043.65**
Date:		

Month Seven

DAY 202

Daily 3% Goal

$1,141.31

Achieved ☐

Piggy Bank Balance

$39,184.96

Date:

DAY 203

Daily 3% Goal

$1,175.55

Achieved ☐

Piggy Bank Balance

$40,360.51

Date:

DAY 204

Daily 3% Goal

$1,210.82

Achieved ☐

Piggy Bank Balance

$41,571.32

Date:

Month Seven

DAY 205 | Daily 3% Goal

$1,247.14

Achieved ☐

Date:

Piggy Bank Balance
$42,818.46

DAY 206 | Daily 3% Goal

$1,284.55

Achieved ☐

Date:

Piggy Bank Balance
$44,103.02

DAY 207 | Daily 3% Goal

$1,323.09

Achieved ☐

Date:

Piggy Bank Balance
$45,426.11

Month Seven

DAY 208 | Daily 3% Goal

$1,362.78

Achieved ☐

Date:

Piggy Bank Balance
$46,788.89

DAY 209 | Daily 3% Goal

$1,403.67

Achieved ☐

Date:

Piggy Bank Balance
$48,192.56

DAY 210 | Daily 3% Goal

$1,445.78

Achieved ☐

Date:

Piggy Bank Balance
$49,638.33

Notes

"Surround yourself with people who will lift you higher."

210 Day

REVIEW

How many days did you reach you Daily Goal?
If you did not reach your goal each day, identify the obstacles you faced.

1.
2.
3.

What action steps need to be taken to overcome the obstacles and get you back on track?

1.
2.
3.

Celebrate Your Victories!
List 1 or 2 things you will do this week to reward yourself for a job well done!

1.
2.

Month Eight

DAY 211	Daily 3% Goal	
	$1,489.15	Piggy Bank Balance
Date:	Achieved ☐	**$51,127.48**

DAY 212	Daily 3% Goal	
	$1,533.82	Piggy Bank Balance
Date:	Achieved ☐	**$52,661.31**

DAY 213	Daily 3% Goal	
	$1,579.84	Piggy Bank Balance
Date:	Achieved ☐	**$54,241.15**

Month Eight

DAY 214	Daily 3% Goal	
	$1,627.23	Piggy Bank Balance
Date:	Achieved ☐	$55,868.38

DAY 215	Daily 3% Goal	
	$1,676.05	Piggy Bank Balance
Date:	Achieved ☐	$57,544.43

DAY 216	Daily 3% Goal	
	$1,726.33	Piggy Bank Balance
Date:	Achieved ☐	$59,270.77

Month Eight

DAY 217	Daily 3% Goal	
	$1,778.12	
Date:	Achieved ☐	Piggy Bank Balance **$61,048.89**

DAY 218	Daily 3% Goal	
	$1,831.47	
Date:	Achieved ☐	Piggy Bank Balance **$62,880.36**

DAY 219	Daily 3% Goal	
	$1,886.41	
Date:	Achieved ☐	Piggy Bank Balance **$64,766.77**

Month Eight

DAY 220 | Daily 3% Goal

$1,943.00

Achieved ☐

Date:

Piggy Bank Balance

$66,709.77

DAY 221 | Daily 3% Goal

$2,001.29

Achieved ☐

Date:

Piggy Bank Balance

$68,711.06

DAY 222 | Daily 3% Goal

$2,061.33

Achieved ☐

Date:

Piggy Bank Balance

$70,772.39

Month Eight

DAY 223	Daily 3% Goal	
	$2,123.17	Piggy Bank Balance
Date:	Achieved ☐	**$72,895.57**

DAY 224	Daily 3% Goal	
	$2,186.87	Piggy Bank Balance
Date:	Achieved ☐	**$75,082.43**

DAY 225	Daily 3% Goal	
	$2,252.47	Piggy Bank Balance
Date:	Achieved ☐	**$77,334.91**

Month Eight

DAY 226 | Daily 3% Goal |
Date: | $2,320.05 | Piggy Bank Balance
 | Achieved ☐ | $79,654.95

DAY 227 | Daily 3% Goal |
Date: | $2,389.65 | Piggy Bank Balance
 | Achieved ☐ | $82,044.60

DAY 228 | Daily 3% Goal |
Date: | $2,461.34 | Piggy Bank Balance
 | Achieved ☐ | $84,505.94

Month Eight

DAY 229	Daily 3% Goal $2,535.18	Piggy Bank Balance $87,041.12
Date:	Achieved ☐	
DAY 230	Daily 3% Goal $2,611.23	Piggy Bank Balance $89,652.35
Date:	Achieved ☐	
DAY 231	Daily 3% Goal $2,689.57	Piggy Bank Balance $92,341.92
Date:	Achieved ☐	

Month Eight

DAY 232 | Daily 3% Goal

$2,770.26

Achieved ☐

Date:

Piggy Bank Balance
$95,112.18

DAY 233 | Daily 3% Goal

$2,853.37

Achieved ☐

Date:

Piggy Bank Balance
$97,965.54

DAY 234 | Daily 3% Goal

$2,938.97

Achieved ☐

Date:

Piggy Bank Balance
$100,904.51

Month Eight

DAY 235 | Daily 3% Goal |
| $3,027.14 |
| Achieved ☐ | Piggy Bank Balance
Date: | | $103,931.65

DAY 236 | Daily 3% Goal |
| $3,117.95 |
| Achieved ☐ | Piggy Bank Balance
Date: | | $107,049.60

DAY 237 | Daily 3% Goal |
| $3,211.49 |
| Achieved ☐ | Piggy Bank Balance
Date: | | $110,261.08

Month Eight

DAY 238 | Daily 3% Goal
$3,307.83

Achieved ☐

Date:

Piggy Bank Balance
$113,568.92

DAY 239 | Daily 3% Goal
$3,407.07

Achieved ☐

Date:

Piggy Bank Balance
$116,975.98

DAY 240 | Daily 3% Goal
$3,509.28

Achieved ☐

Date:

Piggy Bank Balance
$120,485.26

Notes

"Believe you can and you're halfway there."
- Theodore Roosevelt

240 Day
REVIEW

How many days did you reach you Daily Goal?
If you did not reach your goal each day, identify the
obstacles you faced.

1.
2.
3.

What action steps need to be taken to overcome the
obstacles and get you back on track?

1.
2.
3.

Celebrate Your Victories!
List 1 or 2 things you will do this week to reward
yourself for a job well done!

1.
2.

Month Nine

DAY 241	Daily 3% Goal	
	$3,614.56	
Date:	Achieved ☐	**Piggy Bank Balance** $124,099.82

DAY 242	Daily 3% Goal	
	$3,722.99	
Date:	Achieved ☐	**Piggy Bank Balance** $127,822.82

DAY 243	Daily 3% Goal	
	$3,834.68	
Date:	Achieved ☐	**Piggy Bank Balance** $131,657.50

Month Nine

DAY 244	Daily 3% Goal $3,949.72 Achieved ☐	 Piggy Bank Balance $135,607.22
Date:		
DAY 245	Daily 3% Goal $4,068.22 Achieved ☐	 Piggy Bank Balance $139,675.44
Date:		
DAY 246	Daily 3% Goal $4,190.26 Achieved ☐	 Piggy Bank Balance $143,865.70
Date:		

Month Nine

DAY 247

Daily 3% Goal

$4,315.97

Achieved ☐

Date:

Piggy Bank Balance

$148,181.68

DAY 248

Daily 3% Goal

$4,445.45

Achieved ☐

Date:

Piggy Bank Balance

$152,627.13

DAY 249

Daily 3% Goal

$4,578.81

Achieved ☐

Date:

Piggy Bank Balance

$157,205.94

Month Nine

DAY 250 | Daily 3% Goal

$4,716.18

Achieved ☐

Date:

Piggy Bank Balance
$161,922.12

DAY 251 | Daily 3% Goal

$4,857.66

Achieved ☐

Date:

Piggy Bank Balance
$166,779.78

DAY 252 | Daily 3% Goal

$5,003.39

Achieved ☐

Date:

Piggy Bank Balance
$171,783.18

Month Nine

DAY 253 | Daily 3% Goal

$5,153.50

Achieved ☐

Date:

Piggy Bank Balance
$176,936.67

DAY 254 | Daily 3% Goal

$5,308.10

Achieved ☐

Date:

Piggy Bank Balance
$182,244.77

DAY 255 | Daily 3% Goal

$5,467.34

Achieved ☐

Date:

Piggy Bank Balance
$187,712.11

Month Nine

DAY 256 | Daily 3% Goal |

$5,631.36

Achieved ☐

Piggy Bank Balance

$193,343.48

Date:

DAY 257 | Daily 3% Goal |

$5,800.30

Achieved ☐

Piggy Bank Balance

$199,143.78

Date:

DAY 258 | Daily 3% Goal |

$5,974.31

Achieved ☐

Piggy Bank Balance

$205,118.09

Date:

Month Nine

DAY 259 | Daily 3% Goal

$6,153.54

Achieved ☐

Date:

Piggy Bank Balance

$211,271.64

DAY 260 | Daily 3% Goal

$6,338.15

Achieved ☐

Date:

Piggy Bank Balance

$217,609.79

DAY 261 | Daily 3% Goal

$6,528.29

Achieved ☐

Date:

Piggy Bank Balance

$224,138.08

Month Nine

DAY 262 | Daily 3% Goal

$6,724.14

Achieved ☐

Piggy Bank Balance
$230,862.22

Date:

DAY 263 | Daily 3% Goal

$6,925.87

Achieved ☐

Piggy Bank Balance
$237,788.09

Date:

DAY 264 | Daily 3% Goal

$7,133.64

Achieved ☐

Piggy Bank Balance
$244,921.73

Date:

Month Nine

DAY 265	Daily 3% Goal $7,347.65	Piggy Bank Balance $252,269.38
Date:	Achieved ☐	

DAY 266	Daily 3% Goal $7,568.08	Piggy Bank Balance $259,837.47
Date:	Achieved ☐	

DAY 267	Daily 3% Goal $7,795.12	Piggy Bank Balance $267,632.59
Date:	Achieved ☐	

Month Nine

DAY 268	Daily 3% Goal	
	$8,028.98	
	Achieved ☐	Piggy Bank Balance
Date:		$275,661.57

DAY 269	Daily 3% Goal	
	$8,269.85	
	Achieved ☐	Piggy Bank Balance
Date:		$283,931.41

DAY 270	Daily 3% Goal	
	$8,517.94	
	Achieved ☐	Piggy Bank Balance
Date:		$292,449.36

Notes

"One Day, Or Day One, You Decide."

270 Day
REVIEW

How many days did you reach you Daily Goal?
If you did not reach your goal each day, identify the
obstacles you faced.

1.
2.
3.

What action steps need to be taken to overcome the
obstacles and get you back on track?

1.
2.
3.

Celebrate Your Victories!
List 1 or 2 things you will do this week to reward
yourself for a job well done!

1.
2.

$

Month Ten

DAY 271	Daily 3% Goal	
	$8,773.48	
	Achieved ☐	Piggy Bank Balance
Date:		$301,222.84
DAY 272	Daily 3% Goal	
	$9,036.69	
	Achieved ☐	Piggy Bank Balance
Date:		$310,259.52
DAY 273	Daily 3% Goal	
	$9,307.79	
	Achieved ☐	Piggy Bank Balance
Date:		$319,567.31

Month Ten

DAY 274 Date:	Daily 3% Goal $9,587.02 Achieved ☐	 Piggy Bank Balance $329,154.33
DAY 275 Date:	Daily 3% Goal $9,874.63 Achieved ☐	 Piggy Bank Balance $339,028.96
DAY 276 Date:	Daily 3% Goal $10,170.87 Achieved ☐	 Piggy Bank Balance $349,199.83

Month Ten

DAY 277 | Daily 3% Goal

$10,475.99

Achieved ☐

Date:

Piggy Bank Balance
$359,675.82

DAY 278 | Daily 3% Goal

$10,790.27

Achieved ☐

Date:

Piggy Bank Balance
$370,466.10

DAY 279 | Daily 3% Goal

$11,113.98

Achieved ☐

Date:

Piggy Bank Balance
$381,580.08

Month Ten

DAY 280 | Daily 3% Goal

$11,447.40

Achieved ☐

Date:

Piggy Bank Balance

$393,027.48

DAY 281 | Daily 3% Goal

$11,790.82

Achieved ☐

Date:

Piggy Bank Balance

$404,818.31

DAY 282 | Daily 3% Goal

$12,144.55

Achieved ☐

Date:

Piggy Bank Balance

$416,962.85

Month Ten

DAY 283	Daily 3% Goal $12,508.89 Achieved ☐	 Piggy Bank Balance $429,471.74
Date:		
DAY 284	Daily 3% Goal $12,884.15 Achieved ☐	 Piggy Bank Balance $442,355.89
Date:		
DAY 285	Daily 3% Goal $13,270.68 Achieved ☐	 Piggy Bank Balance $455,626.57
Date:		

Month Ten

DAY 286	Daily 3% Goal	
	$13,668.80	
	Achieved ☐	Piggy Bank Balance
Date:		$469,295.37
DAY 287	Daily 3% Goal	
	$14,078.86	
	Achieved ☐	Piggy Bank Balance
Date:		$483,374.23
DAY 288	Daily 3% Goal	
	$14,501.23	
	Achieved ☐	Piggy Bank Balance
Date:		$497,875.45

Month Ten

DAY 289	Daily 3% Goal	
	$14,936.26	
Date:	Achieved ☐	Piggy Bank Balance $512,811.72

DAY 290	Daily 3% Goal	
	$15,384.35	
Date:	Achieved ☐	Piggy Bank Balance $528,196.07

DAY 291	Daily 3% Goal	
	$15,845.88	
Date:	Achieved ☐	Piggy Bank Balance $544,041.95

Month Ten

DAY 292	Daily 3% Goal $16,321.26	
Date:	Achieved ☐	Piggy Bank Balance $560,363.21
DAY 293	Daily 3% Goal $16,810.90	
Date:	Achieved ☐	Piggy Bank Balance $577,174.11
DAY 294	Daily 3% Goal $17,315.22	
Date:	Achieved ☐	Piggy Bank Balance $594,489.33

Month Ten

DAY 295 | Daily 3% Goal

$17,834.68

Achieved ☐

Date:

Piggy Bank Balance
$612,324.01

DAY 296 | Daily 3% Goal

$18,369.72

Achieved ☐

Date:

Piggy Bank Balance
$630,693.73

DAY 297 | Daily 3% Goal

$19,488.44

Achieved ☐

Date:

Piggy Bank Balance
$649,614.54

Month Ten

DAY 298	Daily 3% Goal	
	$19,488.44	Piggy Bank Balance
Date:	Achieved ☐	**$669,102.98**

DAY 299	Daily 3% Goal	
	$20,073.09	Piggy Bank Balance
Date:	Achieved ☐	**$689,176.07**

DAY 300	Daily 3% Goal	
	$20,675.28	Piggy Bank Balance
Date:	Achieved ☐	**$709,851.35**

Notes

"Winners Are Not People Who Never Fail, But People Who Never Quit."

300 Day
REVIEW

How many days did you reach you Daily Goal?
If you did not reach your goal each day, identify the
obstacles you faced.

1.
2.
3.

What action steps need to be taken to overcome the
obstacles and get you back on track?

1.
2.
3.

Celebrate Your Victories!
List 1 or 2 things you will do this week to reward
yourself for a job well done!

1.
2.

Month Eleven

DAY 301 | Daily 3% Goal |
| | Piggy Bank Balance
| $21,295.54 |
| | $731,146.89
| Achieved ☐ |
Date: | |

DAY 302 | Daily 3% Goal |
| | Piggy Bank Balance
| $21,934.41 |
| | $753,081.30
| Achieved ☐ |
Date: | |

DAY 303 | Daily 3% Goal |
| | Piggy Bank Balance
| $22,592.44 |
| | $775,673.73
| Achieved ☐ |
Date: | |

Month Eleven

DAY 304 | Daily 3% Goal

$23,270.21

Achieved ☐

Date:

Piggy Bank Balance
$798,943.95

DAY 305 | Daily 3% Goal

$23,968.32

Achieved ☐

Date:

Piggy Bank Balance
$822,912.26

DAY 306 | Daily 3% Goal

$24,687.37

Achieved ☐

Date:

Piggy Bank Balance
$847,599.63

Month Eleven

DAY 307	Daily 3% Goal $25,427.99	Piggy Bank Balance $873,027.62
Date:	Achieved ☐	

DAY 308	Daily 3% Goal $26,190.83	Piggy Bank Balance $899,218.45
Date:	Achieved ☐	

DAY 309	Daily 3% Goal $26,976.55	Piggy Bank Balance $926,195.00
Date:	Achieved ☐	

Month Eleven

DAY 310 | Daily 3% Goal

$27,785.85

Achieved ☐

Date:

Piggy Bank Balance

$953,980.85

DAY 311 | Daily 3% Goal

$28,619.43

Achieved ☐

Date:

Piggy Bank Balance

$982,600.28

DAY 312 | Daily 3% Goal

$29,478.01

Achieved ☐

Date:

Piggy Bank Balance

$1,012,078.29

You Did It!

$1,000,000

End Of The Year Totals

DAY 330 | Daily 3% Goal

$50,184.34

Achieved ☐

Piggy Bank Balance
$1,722,995.54

Date:

DAY 365 | Daily 3% Goal

$141,211.82

Achieved ☐

Piggy Bank Balance
$4,848,818.45

Date:

MY YEAR END TOTAL

$

Piggy Bank Balance

Date:

Moving Forward

Congratulations on completing *The Millionaire Blueprint*. You are now part of a growing movement of men and women who are *Changing Their Lives* one step at a time. Our mission is to inspire and help millions of people do what you just accomplished: Commit to taking one step, reaching one goal each day to make a breakthrough change in their lives. This is a never ending process.

Our hope is that you will continue to learn, to grow and to make more positive changes in your life and to help others do the same. Your success can provide others with hope that they also can *Change Their Life*. The more you give, the more you will receive. Share what you have learned over the past year and help someone else ***MAKE CHANGE HAPPEN!***

WE WANT TO HEAR YOUR TRANSFORMATION STORY!

We would love to hear from you, so we can answer any questions you may have and see how this Blueprint has helped you transform your life!

If you are interested in more personalized mentorship and group support, consider joining our Inner Circle.

Contact us below for more information!

Email us!
masteringmindset@gmail.com
or
send us a private message on FB or Instagram

Follow us on Social Media:

https://www.facebook.com/changeyourlifevlog

@changeyourlifevlog

www.youtube.com/changeyourlifevlog

www.ChangeYourLifeVlog.com

Made in the USA
Las Vegas, NV
01 October 2023

78385699R00086